WITHDRAWN
FROM STOCK

NORFOLK
FROM THE AIR
A-Z

NORFOLK
FROM THE AIR
A-Z

MIKE PAGE & PAULINE YOUNG

HALSGROVE

First published in Great Britain in 2009
Reprinted 2010

British Library Cataloguing-in-Publication Data
A CIP record for this title is available from the British Library

ISBN 978 1 84114 895 3

HALSGROVE
Halsgrove House,
Ryelands Industrial Estate,
Bagley Road, Wellington, Somerset TA21 9PZ
Tel: 01823 653777   Fax: 01823 216796
email: sales@halsgrove.com

Part of the Halsgrove group of companies
Information on all Halsgrove titles is available at: www.halsgrove.com

Printed and bound in China by Toppan Leefung Printing Ltd

FOREWORD

Mike Page has taken to the skies again, this time to produce a book of aerial pictures covering the whole county. A huge task! But done beautifully. You'll find it so easy from these aerial pictures to see the enormous contrasts in the county's different types of landscape and man's impact on them.

Stretching from the edge of the Fens to the sandy Brecklands, from coast to county boundary, from new roads built on old railway tracks, and from the regimented rows of forestry planting to the variety of foliage colours in an arboretum: all are there in these pages. You'll see also a range of superb aerial views of market towns and isolated villages, historic sites and new developments. Altogether this collection gives the reader a very special birds-eye view of the county from a perspective rarely seen.

Pauline Young's well researched accompanying text provides a miscellany of information that makes this book even more memorable.

James Hoseason OBE
Beccles, 2009

ACKNOWLEDGEMENTS

We are indebted to the following for their help in the preparation of this book: co-pilots Peter Day, Brian Barr, Tim Ball and Alan Green. Also to Richard Adderson, Robert Malster, Shaun Read, the Reverend Colin Way, to Judy Speed our proof reader and as always, our long suffering spouses Gillian Page and John Young.

INTRODUCTION

Deciding on a title for this book was difficult. We thought first about dividing the county into segments much like an orange. But, like dividing an orange, we felt the result would be messy. We then considered producing an 'Aerial Norfolk A-Z' which got closer to what we wanted to achieve, but as there is so much to photograph we couldn't capture every letter, and Z was giving us trouble for ages until Mike suggested a zoo!

And so we settled on *Norfolk from the Air* with the subtitle A-Z, this being exactly what the book portrays. Within these pages there are examples of every type of landscape from the light soils of Breckland to the heavy clays of South Norfolk, from the oldest castles to modern factories, from Broadland waters to Fenland drainage, from magnificent churches to much loved (by some) shopping malls, from ancient tracks to busy road interchanges, and from windmills to windturbines.

Norfolk's all here. Enjoy!

Mike Page
Strumpshaw

Pauline Young
Wymondham

Norfolk Coast and County

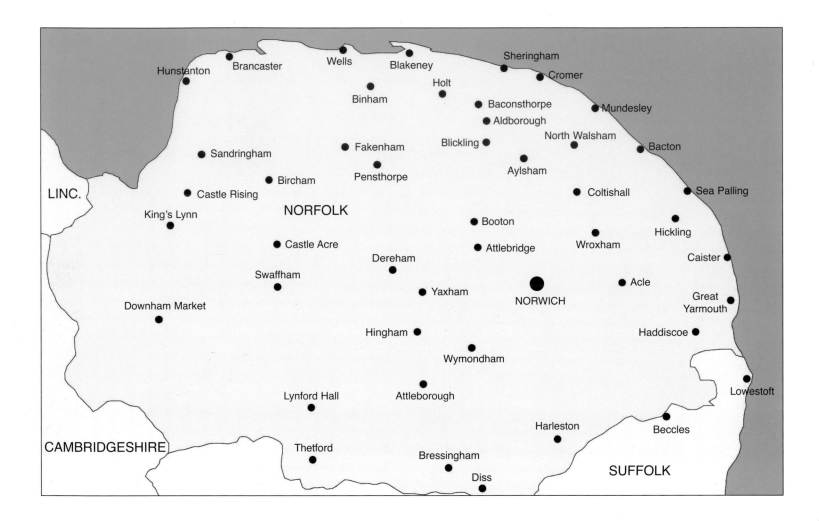

A11 SNETTERTON TOWARDS ATTLEBOROUGH

At last, most of the A11 in Norfolk, the London Road, has been dualled, this stretch only recently. Attleborough is seen in the distance and seven miles further on lies Wymondham. The stretch between the two towns was the first in Norfolk to have a turnpike or toll road. The junction (foreground) shows an industrial estate to the left with Snetterton Race track off picture to the right.

ALDBOROUGH

No longer used for grazing animals, the large common now provides a sports field in this North Norfolk village. In the past, people owning nearby properties and possessing 'common rights' were able to graze their animals. This was 'common' to all those holding such rights hence the name.

Opposite: **A47 ACLE STRAIGHT**

This snowy scene highlights the paths of the River Bure, the A47 'Acle Straight' and the railway. The railway is the line connecting Great Yarmouth and Norwich via Acle. The 'Acle New Road' (new in 1831 and originally a toll road) is part of the A47 which runs between Great Yarmouth and The Midlands. Building a road across marshy ground such as this always has presented problems because without a suitable foundation the road quickly develops undulations. One solution used to be to build the road on a mattress of faggots (bundles of twigs and sticks).

ATTLEBRIDGE

Built in 1941 this airfield was intended to be a satellite to RAF Swanton Morley, both part of Bomber Command. In 1942 the airfield was allocated to the USAAF and subsequently for a short while to a Dutch squadron engaged upon anti-shipping work with Coastal Command. In August 1944 Glenn Miller gave a concert on the airfield, James Stewart was in the audience. The RAF sold the station in 1959, the USAAF having occupied it for most of WW2. Perhaps with the American tradition of roast turkey at the annual Thanksgiving meal it's fairly appropriate that the runways are now used to house turkey sheds!

Opposite: **ALDEBY QUARRY**
Sand and gravel quarry or moonscape?

AYLSHAM

Norfolk Market towns tend to have their parish churches close to their Market Squares. The churchyard here contains the grave of architect and landscape gardener Humphry Repton (1752–1818). It was said he reduced his professional charges when he particularly enjoyed a project. When the Aylsham Navigation (1799) was open wherries came up here on the River Bure which greatly added to the prosperity of the town.

BACONSTHORPE CASTLE

The ancient Bacon family (hence the castle's name) sold their estates here to the Heydon dynasty in the fifteenth century. The Heydons promptly began to build the fortified moated manor or castle around 1450. Only the two gatehouses and the outside walls remain, much of the building was demolished around 1650 when the Heydon family's fortunes declined.

BEESTON BUMP

The triangulation point on the top of the hill says 63 metres. The Norfolk Long Distance Coastpath runs across the top and ends on the approach near Cromer which lies eastwards. As elsewhere on this coast, cliff erosion is an ongoing problem hence the sturdy sea defences.

BERNEY ARMS

This is the tallest drainage mill in Broadland and, unusually, was built to grind clinker for a nearby cement works. It was later converted to marsh drainage. On the opposite bank of the River Yare on The Island stands Raven Hall and Langley Detached Mill – detached from its parish of Langley near Loddon and used for summer grazing. Haddiscoe Island is surrounded by the Rivers Yare and Waveney and on the third side by the New Cut. Within living memory people living on The Island crossed to the 'mainland' by boat and either walked along the sea wall (right) past Breydon Water into Great Yarmouth or walked to the railway station at Berney Arms Halt. The Berney Arms pub is downstream of the mill – Sir John Berney was the local land owner. The marshes on the left are part of the RSPB's Berney marshes reserve.

BINHAM

Before the Reformation destroyed most of the religious establishments there were more than fifty monastic houses in Norfolk, some of them on a grand scale such as the Benedictine monastery in Norwich Cathedral and Binham Priory. Binham was founded by Peter de Valoines, a nephew of William the Conqueror, in 1091. Whilst the monks were dispersed on the order of Henry VIII and much of the building destroyed, the nave of this priory remains in use as the parish church.

Opposite: **BEST BEACH IN NORFOLK (well, one of them): HOLKHAM**

The pines were planted in the 1860s to arrest sand blow from the beach onto arable land. Now the pines, Scots, Corsican and Maritime are fully grown and provide landfall shelter for a host of migratory birds. Among other species there's a resident population of crossbills. The wide sandy beach is never crowded.

BIRCHAM WINDMILL

Great Bircham mill was the first restored (1975) windmill in the county. Built in 1846, parts from other mills were used to refurbish it by the present owner and his wife who is the great granddaughter of a previous nineteenth century miller here. The mill is open to the public during the summer and sells its own ground flour.

BLAKENEY

It's difficult now to imagine ships going out from the quay to fish for cod in Icelandic waters as they did in the reign of Elizabeth I. And even earlier, ships from the Glaven ports of Cley, Wiveton and Blakeney were present at the Siege of Calais 1347. Once the saltmarshes were enclosed by their owners for grazing land, Blakeney's role as a port declined but today it's a picturesque haven for sailing boats with shallow draughts.

BLAKENEY AND THE SALTMARSHES

Samphire, considered a delicacy (but it's an acquired taste) grows on the saltmarshes all along this stretch of coast. Blakeney Point on the opposite side of the channel is a National Nature Reserve.

BLICKLING HALL

The 'jewel in the crown' of the National Trust's East Anglian properties, the house was begun in the early 17th century. The lake and the park were designed by Humphry Repton. Norfolk was largely anti Royalist during the Civil War. Roundhead headquarters were in the Hall, at that time owned by the Hobart family. In another war (WW2) RAF Officers stationed at nearby Oulton airfield were billeted at Blickling and it was claimed that their Commanding Officer occupied Anne Boleyn's bedroom. But four centuries separated them.

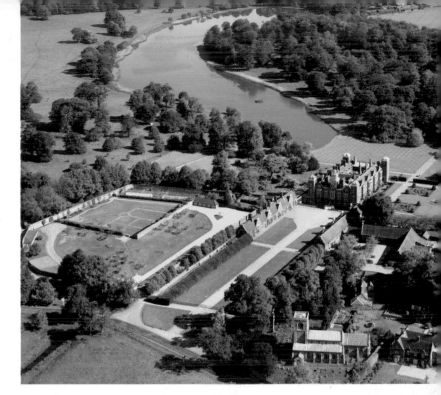

BOOTON CHURCH

Norfolk born, the Reverend Whitwell Elvin acquired the living of Booton in 1849 and a few years later began this Victorian extravaganza or masterpiece depending on how you look at it. The inner walls of the previous church on the site were left standing but everything else was changed as he went along copying features from other ecclesiastical buildings. The whole was paid for by a wealthy friend who sold chunks of her land to a railway company to finance the work. And after all that effort and expense the church is now redundant.

BRESSINGHAM

Garden innovator Alan Bloom, possibly inventor of the island bed, began the nursery at Bressingham Hall in the late 1940s. Today visitors can see the Dell Garden (island beds), Foggy Bottom (heathers and conifers) and on certain days can see a comprehensive collection of steam engines (locomotives, traction engines and a steam driven roundabout) and tour the gardens on a miniature railway. The site includes a Garden Centre.

Opposite: BRANCASTER GOLF COURSE

The Royal West Norfolk Golf Club, established 1892, *must* have the most picturesquely sited course in the whole country with sea and tidal salt marshes all along its northern boundary. Its entrance is marked by two inscribed granite pillars serving as a war memorial. In the foreground is the village of Brancaster Staithe whilst a mile further west is Brancaster village. Mow Creek lies between the staithe and Scolt Head.

BROMHOLM PRIORY, BACTON

The Cluniac order of monks founded a priory here in 1113 and also at Thetford and Castle Acre. The fortunes of the priory improved considerably in 1223 when it claimed to possess a piece of the true cross attracting huge numbers of pilgrims including the Norfolk born Reeve in the 'Canterbury Tales'. The verse 'Piers Plowman' (1330) says 'Bid the rood (cross) of Bromholm bring me out of debt!'

BURGH CASTLE

When what is now Breydon Water was a much wider river estuary, the Romans built their fort Garianonum or Burgh Castle in the first or second century AD. Caister on the opposite bank may also have been a fort supplying the garrison on Hadrian's Wall. The fort also guarded the route from the sea to the local capital at Caistor St Edmund or Caistor next Norwich (Venta Icenorum) – note the different spelling. The Romans built a harbour here whilst after the Norman Conquest a castle (now levelled) was built in the ruins of the Roman fort. In recent years reed has been allowed to encroach into the channel forming a rond which provides an escape for flood water when tides are high.

BURGH NEXT AYLSHAM

A watermill at Burgh was mentioned in the Domesday Book when the course of the River Bure ran further west. There has been a mill on the site since at least the 16th century when Dutch engineers were employed to divert the river and raise its banks enabling a greater fall of water for the mill. Today's mill dates probably from the eighteenth century. The Aylsham Navigation was completed in 1779 when craft could work up the Bure and through five locks including Burgh between Horstead and Aylsham. When the navigation was wrecked by the disastrous floods of 1912, river trade to Aylsham ceased.

BURNHAM THORPE

There's a great deal of Nelson memorabilia on display in the church where his father was rector but The Rectory where Horatio Nelson was born no longer exists. There are seven Burnham parishes all within a mile and a half of one another.

BURSTON STRIKE SCHOOL

The Burston Strike was the longest in history. Teachers Tom and Kitty Higdon caused alienation among school managers when they fought for better conditions for their pupils. They argued that children should not be taken out of school to help with seasonal agricultural work and that the school working environment be improved.

The strike lasted from 1914 until the beginning of WW2 in 1939, the year in which Tom Higdon died. A rival to the village school was set up on the Green next to the church and the Higdons had the support of the major Trade Unions. By 1930 there were equal numbers of children attending the state run village school and the Strike School which is now a museum and an annual rally of trade unionists is held there.

BYLAUGH HALL
Built near Dereham around 1850, a mere hundred years later the house was 'a conspicuous ruin' (Pevsner) following the theft of lead from the roof. It has been rescued and restored and is now a Conference Centre.

CAISTER CASTLE
The castle was built by Sir John Fastolf 1432–5, considered by some to be the inspiration for Shakespeare's Falstaff. Finance for the castle came from ransom money paid for the release of a French knight John Fastolf had captured at Agincourt.

CAISTOR ST EDMUND

In 1928 a pilot flying overhead noticed a distinctive grid pattern among a withered corn crop. Investigation revealed it to be Venta Icenorum now called Caistor St Edmund or Caistor next Norwich, note the spelling which differentiates it from Caister next Yarmouth. It was occupied by the Iceni tribe and was the most prominent town in Norfolk in Roman times. The size of the town diminished in the third century when massive flint walls were built to enclose about thirty acres of it. Extensive excavation followed the find but most of the flint walled buildings were reburied afterwards to preserve them. St Edmund's church sits on the far side of the excavations.

Opposite: **CASTLE ACRE**

The castle was one of the largest in East Anglia. It was built by William de Warenne who came over with William the Conqueror but by 1347 the castle had been abandoned. Left of the castle mound is the site of a Roman town whose earthworks are still visible. Peddars Way runs close by. St James's church (mid picture) sited between the Castle and the Priory, has been dubbed 'the first drive in church'. The drive/ride in aspect is evidenced by a Norman arch shown high in the brickwork of the south chancel wall. This may have been an opening through which knights on horse back could ride for a blessing immediately before battle. Since knights in heavy and cumbersome full armour had to be winched up onto their horses it would have been quite a performance to have to dismount to enter the church and as for kneeling down to pray . . .

CASTLE ACRE PRIORY
Until the Dissolution of the Monasteries by Henry VIII this was one of the great religious houses in Norfolk, second only to the Franciscan Priory at Walsingham.

CASTLE RISING

In the middle of the 12th century, William d'Albini's workmen got to work with a vengeance and produced this wonderful fortified dwelling plus another one at Old Buckenham. It was here in 1330 that Queen Isabella was imprisoned for her involvement with the murder of Edward II but by 1397 the castle had begun to fall into decay. Across the road from the church are almshouses (c1614) whose residents on occasion attend services in their traditional long red cloaks and pointed black hats. Until the Parliamentary Reform Act of 1832 Rising was a 'Rotten Borough' sending two members to represent a very small population. 'Distinguished' MPs included Horace Walpole (a relative of Robert Walpole – England's first Prime Minister) and Samuel Pepys.

COCKLEY CLEY

The name is both curious and picturesque. Cockley is the collective name for a wood frequented by wild birds whilst Cley refers to the area's clayey soil. In the foreground left of picture is a reconstruction of an Iceni village, there was an Iron Age Fort here at the time of Christ. Fiercest of the tribe's leaders was Boadicea. The village lies on the ancient route of the Icknield Way.

COLTISHALL AIRFIELD

From 1940 until 2006, from Spitfire to Jaguar aircraft, RAF Coltishall was a front line defence station. Douglas Bader was stationed here during WW2. Now the airfield is closed and on part of the site a prison may be built but it won't be called HMP Coltishall, the area allocated for housing is to be called 'Badersfield'.

CROMER

The coming of the railways changed Cromer from a small fishing town – Cromer crabs are world famous – into a popular seaside resort. The sea always has been a power to be reckoned with because of the treacherous sand banks a short distance off shore all along this stretch of coast. The first lighthouse was installed in 1680, the present one in 1833, automated in 1990. Previously a light shone out from the 160' high church tower, the highest church tower in Norfolk, as a landmark and warning to shipping. Cromer's Henry Blogg served on the lifeboat for fifty-three years and was coxswain for thirty-eight of them. He remains the most highly decorated lifeboatman in history. The lifeboat shed at the end of the pier houses the new Tamar class lifeboat 'Lester' which was launched on September 8 2008.

Opposite: **COSTESSEY PARK (COSSEY HALL)**

Cossey Hall is one of the 'lost houses' of Norfolk. Sadly there are many more. All that remains is this fragment, believed to be the Bell Tower, near the eighteenth hole of Costessey Park golf course. The house was mainly sixteenth century in origin but with nineteenth century additions. It was demolished after WWI.

COUNTY BOUNDARY

Geldeston (Norfolk) and Shipmeadow (Suffolk) are divided by the River Waveney which for much of its length forms the county boundary. This is the end of navigation, marked by the replacement bridge seen here being installed. Until 1935 wherries could work up through five locks from Ellingham to Bungay. The remains of Geldeston lock chamber is abeam The Locks pub.

DENVER MILL

Denver's cream coloured tower (1835) is a departure from the usual black tar paint. With six floors it's one of the taller mills. It's open all year round and sells its own flour. The distinctive cap is not unique but it makes a pretty picture.

DENVER SLUICE

Water management always has been a major concern in this fertile low lying area particularly when landowners – especially the Duke of Bedford and entrepreneurs known as the 'Great Adventurers' – began to drain the land for agriculture. Dutch engineers, who in the 17th century already were experts in the subject in their own country, were brought over to give a major overhaul to the system. To Cornelius Vermuyden and subsequently John Rennie goes much of the credit. Artificial rivers – the Forty Foot (width) and the Hundred Foot Drain or New Bedford River – were dug leading from the Old Bedford River to connect with the River Great Ouse flowing out to sea at Kings Lynn. The original Denver Sluice was constructed in 1651 to control the flow of water coming from the Ely direction. A relief or 'Cut Off' channel is parallel to the Great Ouse to take surplus water out to sea at Kings Lynn. This whole area is known as the Middle Level.

The River Great Ouse flows past the sailing club (top) and under the sluice gates towards Kings Lynn. The New Bedford River is off picture (top left). The Cut Off Channel is in the foreground.

DEREHAM

Officially named East Dereham there's more to this mid Norfolk market town than is immediately apparent. Poet and depressive William Cowper (pron. Cooper) (1731–1800) among whose best known work is the narrative tale of John Gilpin and the hymn 'God moves in a mysterious way', written when a suicide attempt failed, is buried here. The birthplace of writer George Borrow is at Dumpling Green a mile away. And Bishop Edmund Bonner, possibly the most hated cleric in the land because of the zeal with which he burned heretics, lived here in a pretty cottage, which still stands, whilst he was Rector of Dereham 1534–38.

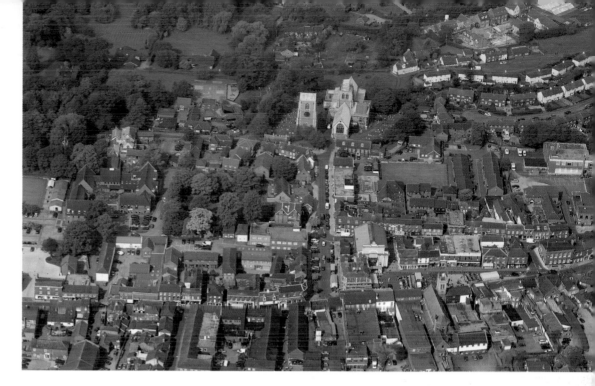

DEREHAM MALTINGS

Malting barley for the brewing industry has long been an important arable crop in Norfolk. Many towns and larger villages within the county had their maltings. This one dates from the 1880s. The grain was first soaked to facilitate germination then spread across the floor hence the building's large size. Before the process became mechanized the grain was turned with traditional wooden shovels to obtain even germination. Germination was halted by subsequent kiln drying. The four 'chimneys' at the ends of the buildings are the original drying kilns. The Mid Norfolk Railway (once upon a time the LNER) from Dereham to Wymondham runs alongside. Much of the malt would have been sent from here by rail.

DISS

Meres are a feature of the county from Breckland southwards and were the sites round which the earliest settlements arose. 'Diss' is from the Anglo Saxon 'dice' meaning 'standing water'. Diss Mere covers six acres and is sixty feet deep in places. Diss's prosperity arose from the fact that it has been a resting place between Norwich and Ipswich over the centuries and a market town into the bargain. Anxious to preserve the beauty and tranquility of the town it was stipulated that the railway line, the main line to London, should be built at least a mile away from the town centre.

DOWNHAM MARKET

The artificial cut (top of picture) which is the New Bedford River and the River Great Ouse run parallel most of the way to Kings Lynn. Considerable quantities of Romano-British pottery have been found near the river indicating that this was an important farming area. Downham's most famous son (he was born at Denver but received his education at Downham) is George Manby, inventor of the device which saved the lives of thousands of shipwrecked sailors. A mortar with a rope attached was fired over a stranded vessel which led to the development of the rocket fired lifeline.

DUNSTON HALL

The central building with numerous chimneys is the original, the rest has been added skillfully to make a coherent whole. It was built around 1880 possibly by local architect Edward Boardman Senior. In the last thirty years the building has changed ownership several times but is now an established Hotel and Conference Venue with Golf Course.

EAST BARSHAM

East Barsham Manor is the picture book ideal of a Tudor House (so says Pevsner). It was built by Sir Henry Fermor around 1520. Henry VIII is said to have lodged here for a night before making a pilgrimage to Walsingham.

EAST RUSTON: THE OLD VICARAGE GARDEN

In the early 1970s this was a windswept two-acre site with a house which had been unoccupied for two years. Today it extends to thirty-two acres of wonderful themed gardens of variety, richness and innovation. These include Dutch, Jungle, Californian, Dry River Bed, Sunken, Exotic, Mediterranean, Vegetable and Cutting Gardens. A vista of Happisburgh Lighthouse is particularly striking as is the huge variety of plants and trees. Shelter belts planted with reference to the OS map of the 1880s give protection from the biting east wind.

If you're not a gardener or plant lover before you visit, by the time you leave you will be!

FAKENHAM

Which other town can boast both a National Hunt racecourse and a Gas Museum! Fakenham was the last remaining town to have its own gas works. They closed in 1965 since when the equipment has been preserved in the Museum. With the exception of the War Years the racecourse has been holding regular meetings since 1905, one of its most loyal and enthusiastic supporters was HM the Queen Mother. Both the Great Eastern railway from Dereham to Wells and the M & GN from Kings Lynn to Melton Constable served the town. Now there are no railways routeing through Fakenham.

FAKENHAM TOWN CENTRE

A typical Norfolk market town, it's a pity the church is hidden behind houses at ground level. Below the church clock are grids or 'sound holes' for the bells . In the Market Place the former rectangular red brick and stone Corn Exchange was latterly a cinema whilst the solid grey brick edifice is still a bank. Near the War Memorial in Market Square is the Crown Inn which the first Thomas Cook, originator of Cook's Tours, frequented when on his visits to Norfolk. It was, allegedly, one of his less commendable habits to heat a shovelful of copper coins in the inn's fire, toss them red hot into the street and watch little boys burn their fingers as they scrambled for them.

FELBRIGG

The Hall could almost be described as 'cosily domestic' compared to other stately houses in the county. It was begun before the Civil War and added to over the centuries. Bought by John Ketton in 1863, it fell into disrepair due to the extravagances of family member 'Mad Windham' who, for a wager, opted to drive the Cromer to Norwich Stage Coach at full pelt through the North Norfolk villages. The Hall was restored by the Ketton Cremers in 1923 but when the last of the line died the estate was left to the National Trust. There are five hundred and twenty acres of woods and waymarked trails and a fine walled garden. The stables (right of the complex) now houses a shop, second-hand bookshop, restaurant and tea shop.

FORESTRY COMMISSION WOODLAND

The Forestry Commission was established in 1921 and it immediately purchased large areas of land in Breckland in order to maintain the nation's timber supplies. Pines were hand planted in their thousands together with a rabbit eradication programme to ensure the trees' survival. Later planting schemes favoured the larger Corsican pines with strips of native hardwoods along roadsides for aesthetic reasons.

Opposite: FOWLMERE AND THE BRECKS

There are at least nine meres (naturally formed lakes) within Breckland but most are in the Battle Area where the Army has sealed off hundreds of acres for military manoeuvres. Between Fowlmere (the larger of the two meres) and the Devil's Punchbowl (the smaller) runs an ancient Drove road. The water level of the meres rises and falls with the underlying water table because each is lying on the chalk strata. Forestry Commission plantings with their straight rows and blocks of trees abound but it was the rabbit population which made the most impact on the landscape until a hundred years or so ago. Rabbits and sheep were the only creatures which could survive on the thin sandy soils. And within living memory rabbit pelts were used in the making of top hats in the small market town of Brandon. The Norwich and Ely railway line is top of picture. The term Breckland was coined as recently as 1894 by naturalist and journalist W G Clarke when writing about the Brecks which are areas of intermittently cultivated heath-land.

GREAT HAUTBOIS (pron. 'hobbis')

With their usual zeal and energy the Victorians 'ruinated' this hundreds of years old church before building a fresh one on a more conspicuous site in the village. The ruin looks more impressive from the air than on the ground.

Opposite: **GREAT YARMOUTH OUTER HARBOUR**

2009 sees the completion of the first phase of the Outer Harbour. Since Yarmouth is the principal base for oil and gas extraction in the southern part of the North Sea the new harbour should breathe new life into the surrounding area. The South Denes is an ideal site with space for sheds, warehouses etc. and provision for new quays. The river can accommodate vessels of six metres' draught, the new harbour is being dredged to a depth of ten metres. Everything is set fair for an upturn in Yarmouth's fortunes. There's just one snag – the A47 which is the main commercial route to the Midlands, has between Yarmouth and Acle (the Acle Straight) only one lane in either direction. Calls for the road to be enlarged have so far come to nothing. Which will come first – dualling the Acle Straight or finding King John's jewels in The Wash?

GRESSENHALL

Originally a Union Workhouse (so called because it served a union of several adjacent parishes) Gressenhall is now a splendid museum run by Norfolk County Council whose Archaeological Unit is based here too. Just how awful being sent to the workhouse must have been is well illustrated by the displays, room scenes and commentaries within the building.

GRIMES GRAVES

Aerial photography really comes into its own here! For many years these peculiar depressions (bell pits) were thought to be prehistoric burial chambers but excavations in 1870 revealed them to be flint mines. The Belgic Celts introduced flint mining into Britain. This extremely hard stone was used for axe heads for clearing land for example. The height of mining activity was around 2000BC but gun flints were being produced in large quantities at the time of the Napoleonic Wars and even as late as the 1950s flint knapping (splitting the flint to reveal the rich colours of the interior) was a common trade in Breckland especially around Brandon. Many Norfolk and Suffolk churches have fine examples of knapped flintwork whilst the use of flint cobbles as a building material is very much in evidence in Norfolk.

GRIMSTON WARREN
The Romans and the Iceni almost certainly inhabited this area but by its very name the most numerous population would have been rabbits. They were farmed as a cash crop until a couple of centuries ago and 'Warren' place names crop up all over Breckland.

GUNTON HALL

This extraordinarily large range of buildings was begun by Matthew Brettingham in 1742 and added to by James Wyatt 1785. Parts were derelict or fire damaged when award winning restoration began and now twenty-one years later a white elephant has been turned into a score of elegant houses.

GUNTON PARK

A curious Observatory Tower, probably Victorian, was later added, sited in the parkland. It too is now a dwelling.

59

HADDISCOE CHURCH

There are more round tower churches in Norfolk (one hundred and seventy) than in any other county (Suffolk is second). There are differing opinions as to why the round tower was so common in early churches. Square flint towers need corner stones and for ages it was thought that a lack of local stone necessitated towers being built in the round and the plentiful flint cobble was the obvious material. But on investigation it was discovered that there are plenty of round towers in West Norfolk where the local carr stone would have served as corner stones. There are round towered churches in every country where the Vikings settled and they had the technology to build square towers with flint corners. Another theory is that round towers were built as defences. We just don't know. Haddiscoe church tower with its later addition of a chequered and crenellated top is certainly one of the 'prettiest' round towers in Norfolk.

Opposite: **HADDISCOE ISLAND**

One advantage of snowy ground is that rivers, roads and railways stand out! Here the River Yare (left) and the River Waveney (right) meet in Breydon Water. The railway (1847) between Lowestoft and Norwich and Reedham runs parallel to the New Cut (new in the 1830s). The coming of the railway was largely responsible for the commercial failure of the New Cut as an efficient way of transporting goods from Lowestoft to Norwich thereby avoiding Yarmouth Harbour dues. At times of extreme water rise today the Cut overflows and floods the railway line thereby extracting a sort of vengeance on its old rival!

HALES

The present group of buildings are part of a once larger site. Hales Court (now known as Hales Hall) was built for Sir James Hobart, Attorney General to Henry VII. The magnificent barn with its stepped gables is one hundred and eighty four feet long. The principal hall block is long gone.

Opposite: **HAPPISBURGH**

Everyone who has a TV set will recently have seen the plight of the cliffs at Happisburgh, they're eroding very fast. How long will it be before the lighthouse and the church tumble into the sea? – it's happened before on this stretch of coast! The churchyard contains the graves of shipwrecked sailors from several centuries including thirty two men from HMS 'Peggy' 1770 which ran aground on the treacherous sands which are strung out just off shore all along this stretch of the coast. Buried here also are all hands of HMS 'Hunter' wrecked 1804, one hundred and nineteen seamen from HMS 'Invincible' lost on Hammond Knoll in 1801 when sailing to join the fleet at Copenhagen, twelve men from the barque 'Young England' wrecked 1876 and, more recently, three German airmen shot down in WW2.

HARLESTON

This small town on the border of Norfolk and Suffolk is somewhat fragmented by the very necessary one way traffic system. Originally the Market Place occupied the entire central area but was later infilled with dwellings. The town contains elegant Georgian buildings and a couple of older pubs. 'The Swan' was frequented by Sir Alfred Munnings who was born and lived in nearby Mendham Mill.

HICKLING

Reed fringed Hickling is the largest broad and one of the quieter because of the height restriction for boats passing under the mediaeval Potter Heigham bridge. It has been a sailor's paradise – except for the year when a rare weed choked the broad. Areas around the broad have intriguing names such as 'Swim Coots', 'Rush Hills' and 'Deep Go Dyke'. Many a royal bottom has sat on the benches in the hides waiting to bag a water bird or two. Reed is harvested by the Norfolk Wildlife Trust who are custodians of some of the marshes and whose Information Centre and boardwalks are ever popular with human visitors. The proximity to the coastline reveals the vulnerability of the area from invasion by the sea.

HINGHAM

Hingham's wide main street and elegant Georgian houses add up to an attractive village whose main claim to fame is that Abraham Lincoln's forebears set sail from England to America and founded a colony they named Hingham in Massachusetts. A curiosity in the main street is a mounting block to assist riders onto their horses.

Opposite: **HOLKHAM**

Holkham, built by Thomas Coke (pronounced Cook and not to be confused with Thomas Cook and his mansion Sennowe Park at Guist), employed William Kent and subsequently Norfolk's own Matthew Brettingham to build the Hall. The landscaping, including the planting of thousands of trees and the creation of an artificial lake by damming a creek, was planned by Coke himself. He made Holkham prosperous by improving the land including the planting of a belt of trees at the shoreline to mitigate the effects of wind erosion. He turned an area where once 'two rabbits fought for one blade of grass' into fertile farmland. His great nephew and namesake 'Coke of Norfolk' later to become the Earl of Leicester followed in his forebear's footsteps and proved to be one of the greatest innovators in crop and live-stock husbandry.

HOLT

An extensive fire in 1708 resulted in the rebuilding of a large number of houses in the Georgian era. Holt is considered one of the most attractive small market towns in Norfolk. It's also the western terminus of the North Norfolk Railway and was once part of the Midland and Great Northern or 'Muddle and Get Nowhere' railway.

HOLT: GRESHAM'S SCHOOL

Holt resident and financier Thomas Gresham (1519–79) founded the Royal Exchange at his own expense. He established a school in his own house in Holt's Market Place offering free education to thirty scholars and entrusting the running of it to the Worshipful Company of Fishmongers. Now a Public School, mostly the education gained there is far from free! Old boys include Benjamin Britten, W H Auden, Lord Reith (founder of the BBC), Sir Christopher Cockerell (inventor of the Hovercraft) and Stephen Fry.

HOUGHTON HALL

The Hall was built by England's first Prime Minister Robert Walpole around 1720 at a cost almost as great as Blenheim Palace so that when Walpole died the estate was so debt ridden that the pictures had to be sold. They were bought by Catherine the Great and are now part of the Hermitage collection in St Petersburg. Houghton and Holkham are said to be the two most spectacular Palladian houses in Norfolk but Houghton became close to being a ruin after WW2. It was rescued by Sybil, Dowager Marchioness of Cholmondeley. White deer roam the park.

HUNSTANTON AND THE WASH

On a clear day the Lincolnshire coast and Boston Stump (church tower) can be seen across The Wash. Old Hunstanton is in the foreground with the larger holiday resort of New Hunstanton, made fashionable by royal patronage, a mile or so further on. The channel to Kings Lynn is top left. Before sea levels rose there was a treacherous causeway across The Wash to what is now Lincolnshire.

HUNSTANTON CLIFFS

A mecca for fossil collectors, the cliff layers from the top downwards are glacial deposits of white chalk, red ironstone and yellow carrstone. The chalk runs in a seam all the way to the Chilterns. This was a favourite picnic spot for King Edward VII and Queen Alexandra when staying at Sandringham. The rocks provided both a table on which a servant could lay a cloth and set out food and a seat for the King who could sit and smoke a cigar whilst contemplating this very special part of his kingdom.

HUNSTANTON HALL

Home of the Le Strange family, the moated Hall in Old Hunstanton was begun in 1500 and added to over the centuries. Hamon Le Strange supported the Royalist cause during the Civil War and was involved in the Siege of Kings Lynn. Entrepreneur Henry LeStrange is credited with the development of New Hunstanton as a resort.

KELLING HEATH

Now an area of outstanding beauty, previously smugglers would cross the heath with their contraband. Now it's crossed instead by the North Norfolk Railway and so, in the distance, does the road from Weybourne to Holt.

KINGS LYNN

Kings Lynn originally was called Bishops Lynn and in the possession of the bishopric of Norwich. Many of the town's mediaeval buildings have been destroyed for redevelopment but thankfully the splendid Custom House (1683) remains on the Purfleet Quay. The Custom House represents the importance of sea-going trade to the town. The statue is of Captain George Vancouver (Lynn born 1757) who left his name on the map of Canada after exploring and charting the west coast of that country.

LETHERINGSETT MILL

This is the only remaining working watermill in Norfolk. It's unusual in that it works breastshot in normal mode or undershot if water levels in the River Glaven become low. A mill on the site was mentioned in the Domesday Book but the present one was built in 1802. Flour can still be bought on the premises.

Opposite: **KINGS LYNN**

Ships from the Baltic ports bringing in timber and ships taking out grain have worked along the River Great Ouse to and from Kings Lynn port for centuries. A new straight and safer course for the river between Lynn and The Wash was cut in the mid nineteenth century. The area is an important wildlife haven especially for sea and wading birds. A foot ferry works across the river providing a short cut to West Lynn.

LYNFORD HALL & ARBORETUM

The Hall was begun in 1856 and took seven years to build. The neo-Jacobean style perfectly suits the site, the modern wing sits a little less pleasingly. The whole is now an hotel and function venue.

The Arboretum's nucleus is the parkland surrounding the house. The Forestry Commission extended the planting with trainee foresters doing much of the work in the 1940s. The 'Friends of Thetford Forest' organization now tends the two hundred different species of broad-leaved and coniferous trees which centre upon the double row of sequoias planted in honour of the Duke of Wellington before the house was built. There's no charge for admission to the Arboretum's walks.

Opposite: LEZIATE COUNTRY PARK

The extraction of silica sand for glass making created the lakes which, in common with many of the sand and gravel extractions in the county, are now used for leisure pursuits particularly dinghy sailing. There's also a Country Club on the site.

Norfolk place names containing the letter z are rare. In the Domesday Book Leziate is 'Lesiet' meaning the gate of a meadow.

MANNINGTON HALL

The moated and crenellated flint hall was built around 1450. Both digging the moat and the crenellation would have required the King's permission. It's fed from a tributary of the River Bure. The lake in the background was dug in the 18th century. Horatio Walpole, brother of the Robert who was England's first Prime Minister, bought the house in 1736. The house was extended by another Walpole, the Earl of Orford, in the nineteenth century. Orford was a misogynist and after his wife left him he decorated the house with comments on the perfidy of women. Walpoles live at Mannington to this day.

MELTON CONSTABLE HALL

The splendour that was once Melton Constable Hall was resurrected in part when the hall was used as a setting for the film ''The Go Between''. Norfolk man L P Hartley wrote the novel from which the film script came. For several hundred years the Hall was owned by the Astley family whose best known member was soldier Sir Jacob Astley. Before going into battle on behalf of King Charles I at Edgehill in 1642, the first battle of the Civil War, Sir Jacob prayed the now familiar 'Oh Lord, Thou knowest how busy I must be this day, if I forget Thee do not Thou forget me.' The Hall was begun in 1664 and took twenty years to build.

MIDDLETON TOWERS

It's quite difficult to spot the genuinely old from the reconstructed. Here's a 15th century fortified manor house but only the turreted three storeyed tower belongs to the 14th century. The rest dates from around 1860. It's a copy of a Tudor mansion but so skillfully done that it looks authentic. The creator of the original Middleton Towers, Lord Scales, was the author of the first book printed in England by Caxton. He wrote some of the Paston Letters – a record of political and domestic life in England in the 15th century.

MUNDESLEY

With the coming of the railway in 1898 this little village became a popular holiday resort and although the railway stopped running in 1964 Mundesley's popularity remains. 'Coastwatch' occupy the square building on top of the cliffs. The 'golf ball' of RAF Trimingham's radar station is on the horizon.

NARFORD HALL

The Hall was begun around 1702 for MP Andrew Fountaine and has remained in the family ever since. A later addition is the Main Entrance which has a grand domed tower.

NESTLÉ SITE 1994

There had been a chocolate factory on this site in the middle of Norwich since 1880. Originally it traded as Caleys and produced the famous 'marching chocolate' found in WWI soldiers' kitbags and now once more available. The firm was taken over by Mackintosh of Halifax in 1932 but the Caley brand name was kept until the 1960s. In 1969 there was a merger with Rowntree and in 1988 Nestlé acquired the firm, closing it in 1994. Throughout its life as a chocolate factory, with the exception of the war years when it was bombed, a wonderful aroma of chocolate used to percolate the city streets.

NESTLÉ SITE 2007

In 2005 the site emerged as the Chapelfield Shopping Mall and flats. One of its Main Entrances opens onto St Stephen's Street. It's claimed that the design of the site was 'inspired by the local architecture' but it's unlikely that much of St Stephen's 1960s brutalist style (the street was badly bombed during WW2 and rebuilt) offered much inspiration.

NEW BUCKENHAM
The castle was removed from Old Buckenham and rebuilt in New Buckenham about 1136. The motte, although now almost completely surrounded by trees, can be seen in the foreground. It was one of ten castles including Castle Acre built at this time. The castles were placed strategically to consolidate Norman rule over the local population. The village was a planned town so entitled 'New' to distinguish it from its more haphazardly created neighbour Old Buckenham.

NORTH ELMHAM

The Saxon Cathedral is among the earliest Christian buildings in Norfolk. It dates from the thirteenth century. The Bishop's See (Diocese) was first here, then at Thetford and finally at Norwich where it is today. The building was surrounded by a moat and there is evidence that part of the building was Bishop Despencer's house. The church next door was begun in the fourteenth century but has been subjected to many alterations.

Inset: **NORTH ELMHAM**
The Saxon cathedral close up

87

NORTH PICKENHAM WINDFARM
The wind turbines were erected on the wartime airfield in 2006, eight of them standing 125m high to the tip of a rotor blade.

Opposite: **NORTH NORFOLK SALT MARSH**
These are surreal patterns and hues. The orange areas may be the result of ochre staining from ferrous oxide in the underlying soil reacting with falling water levels.

NORTH WALSHAM

The tower of St Nicholas parish church suffered a partial collapse in 1724 and has never been rebuilt which might just be considered to be inertia. But on the other hand the townspeople a century and a half later inhabited a town with *three* railway lines (the GER, the Norfolk and Suffolk Joint Railway and the M & GN) and a canal (The North Walsham and Dilham). This indicates rather a lot of trade and work for a small town. Next to the church is the market cross rebuilt after a fire in 1602 so some repairs around the town did get done!

Opposite: NORTH WALSHAM TO THE COAST

Today North Walsham has one working railway line. The Bittern Line from Norwich to Cromer and Sheringham is the former Great Eastern Line which runs almost horizontally across the middle of the picture and parallel to the A149 Yarmouth Road with the railway station mid picture. The line of trees running south westwards is the site of the old M & GN to Melton Constable and Great Yarmouth whose station was called North Walsham Town when the railways were nationalized in 1948. It was near the Bittern Line station but closed in 1959. The third line (the Norfolk & Suffolk Joint Railway) ran northwards to Mundesley then along the coast to Cromer. The Mundesley to Cromer section closed in 1953 but the North Walsham to Mundesley section remained open until 1964.

NORWICH AIRPORT

Scheduled services link Norfolk to the continent as well as to other parts of Britain whilst charter flights operate mainly in the summer months. Originally this was RAF Horsham St Faith built 1940. Taking off from here on a bombing raid in August 1941 a Blenheim aircraft dropped a pair of artificial legs over St Omer Airfield for the use of P.O.W. Wing Commander Douglas Bader.

Opposite: **NORWICH**

The River Wensum and the city walls, enclosing both the Castle and the Cathedral, together provided a good defence against invaders. The growth of the city outwards is demonstrated by the relatively newer advent of Thorpe railway station and Norwich City's football ground. Although retail parks and new roads abound, the heart of the city is compact and despite bomb damage it contains a huge number of historic buildings.

NORWICH CASTLE

There was a small hill here until the Normans got to work, built the mound and surrounded it with a defensive ditch part of which is now the Castle Gardens. The original Caen stone was replaced with harder Bath stone in the nineteenth century giving the keep a less mellow appearance. The keep is now a Museum and a shopping mall is built on the castle bailey which was a cattle market in living memory. The hole dug during the Mall's construction was at the time the deepest artificial hole in Europe and could be depicted from satellite pictures. A jaundiced (male) shopper pointed out recently that 'mall' is pronounced to rhyme with 'appall'.

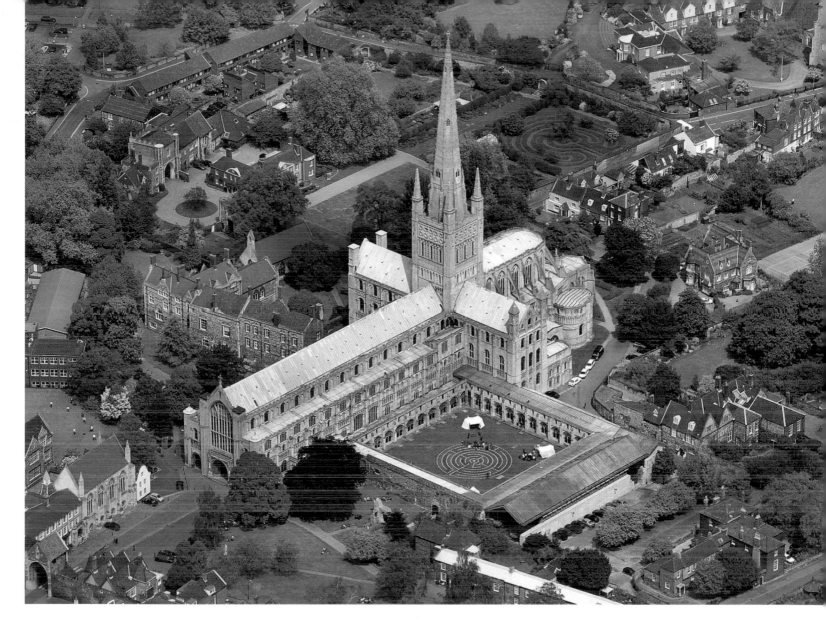

NORWICH CATHEDRAL

Begun 1096, ten years after Domesday Book was compiled, this magnificent edifice was built of stone from Caen in Normandy and Barnack in Northamptonshire. Transported in both cases by water, boats came the final few hundred yards from the watergate at Pulls Ferry into The Close. Mainly open to the elements, the Cloisters are as cold and draughty today as they were when monks made their way along them to services.

ON WROXHAM BROAD

Of all the hundreds of wherries built only eight remain afloat. Here are 'White Moth' (left of picture) a wherry yacht built by Ernest Collins 1915, pleasure wherry 'Ardea' (centre) built 1927 by Robinsons of Oulton Broad and pleasure wherry 'Solace' (right) built 1903 by Halls of Reedham.

   The other wherries afloat are traders 'Albion' (1898) and 'Maud' (1899), pleasure wherry 'Hathor' (1905), wherry yacht 'Olive' (1909) and wherry yacht 'Norada' (1912). 'Ardea' was brought back to The Broads in 2005 having been used as a houseboat in France for many years. Unless another is discovered in restorable condition, 'Ardea' will be the last wherry to join the fleet on The Broads.

OXBURGH HALL

Oxburgh has been described 'the most exciting mediaeval house in Norfolk'. Begun in 1482 it has been lived in by the Bedingfield or Bedingfeld family ever since. Henry VII stayed there and Mary Queen of Scots left her embroidery which was made into wall hangings. The whole has a cosily domestic feel to it despite the Priest's Hole and all that the need to hide a priest implies during the time that Roman Catholics suffered religious persecution.

Left: PEDDARS WAY

The origins of the name are obscure. This ancient track runs from the Suffolk border to Norfolk's north west coast where it joins with the Norfolk Coast Path near Hunstanton. Possibly built and certainly *used* by the Romans around AD61 (the date of Boudica's revolt) evidence of Roman settlements have been found along its length. Mediaeval pilgrims en route to Walsingham walked the Way and cattle and sheep were driven to market along it. It's possible that Peddars Way continued as a causeway across The Wash until the nineteenth century.

Right: PENSTHORPE

These gravel pits in the valley of the River Wensum make an ideal Waterfowl Park. There's one of the world's largest collections of endangered and exotic waterbirds here. In 2008 and 2009 the Park was host to the BBC programme 'Springwatch'.

PULHAM AIRSHIP HANGARS

Pulham Air Station – official title No 2 Coastal Airship Station – was commissioned in 1916 as a base for non rigid airships patrolling the North Sea. The airships affectionately known as 'Pulham Pigs' got their nickname when one Pulham inhabitant on seeing an airship above him remarked "Thet luk loike a gret ol' pig"! After WWI it became an experimental station with both parachute trials and experiments in launching fighter aircraft from beneath the big rigid airship the R33. Fame came when the Pulham based R34 made a both ways crossing of the Atlantic in 1919. The airship was only the second craft of any kind to make a non stop crossing of the Atlantic west to east – the first was Alcock and Brown's Vickers Vimy. During WW2 Pulham was a direction finding radio station. Number One Shed was dismantled in 1948. Number Two Shed still stands at Cardington, sister station to Pulham. In 1958 the RAF Station closed and the land on which it stood was sold in 1962.

PULHAM MARKET WORKHOUSE

Workhouses were sometimes euphemistically called 'Pauper Palaces' but palatial they most certainly were not. The regime was strict and uncomfortable. This was a Union workhouse, built in 1836 for twenty-one parishes and could accommodate four hundred people. The building has been converted to modern flats.

QUIDENHAM

Quidenham Hall became a Carmelite Monastery for nuns in 1984. Because of her books and TV appearances its best known occupant is art historian Sister Wendy Beckett who lives under the protection of the Carmelite nuns. In the smaller buildings at the rear are the premises of the Norfolk part of the East Anglian Children's Hospice organization (EACH) established here in 1985. EACH has also children's hospices at Ipswich (Suffolk) and Milton (Cambridgeshire). The Quidenham Hospice has strong local support, a proportion of the profits from our previous books has been donated to this cause.

RACING ON HICKLING
Norfolk Dinghies taking advantage of the breeze.

RAF MARHAM

RAF Marham started life as Royal Naval Air Station Narborough in 1915. Narborough was designed as a night flying landing station for the RNAS based on the South Denes at Great Yarmouth. Narborough closed in 1919 but in 1935 the area of the air station was encompassed by the creation of RAF Marham, the only active RAF airfield in Norfolk. Tornadoes are based there today as well as an engineering unit and other support functions.

RANWORTH AND MALTHOUSE BROADS

Climb the narrow winding stone staircase and from the top of Ranworth's St Helen's church there's a view almost as good as this one! Malthouse and Ranworth Broads connect by a narrow channel – out of bounds to any craft except the ferry which runs between Malthouse Staithe and the Norfolk Wildlife Trust's floating Information Centre on Ranworth.

Malthouse Staithe is a popular place to moor and visit the shop, the Broads' Information centre or the Maltsters Pub which was a watering hole for wherrymen bringing barley to the malthouse. The pub's sign shows the maltsters shovelling barley grains.

RAYNHAM HALL

The Hall, built for Sir Roger Townshend, dates from 1622 and it's possible that Inigo Jones designed it. For such a monumental undertaking lime and brick kilns were made, roads created, iron was shipped in through Wells and stone through Kings Lynn. A stretch of water was a device often employed to enhance the view from a house. Here the River Wensum, enlarged to form a lake, serves the purpose.

REEDHAM FERRY

In the absence of a road bridge between Norwich and Great Yarmouth the Reedham Ferry is the only means by which vehicles can cross the River Yare.

Opposite: **RIVER GLAVEN VALLEY**

The valley was a wide estuary before the 17th century embankment of the saltmarshes. The tides were then prevented from scouring the navigable channels and the river mouth silted up. Previously ships tied up alongside Wiveton church (left), there are marks to prove it in the churchyard walls. Cley on the opposite bank suffered exactly the same fate, all of its maritime trade was taken away.

SALLE (pron. 'Saul') CHURCH

Norfolk has some of the most splendid churches in the country. Almost a thousand were built between the 11th and 16th centuries and there were six hundred still in use at the end of the 20th century. This one was built in the 15th century thanks to the generosity of three local families of landed gentry. Dedicated to Saints Peter and Paul it's one of the finest examples of the perpendicular style and has been described as a 'near cathedral'.

SANDRINGHAM

Queen Victoria bought the house in 1861 for the heir to the throne, later King Edward VII. It cost £220,000 with 7,000 acres and was a modest dwelling compared to the splendour of some of Norfolk's country houses. In 1870 the Prince of Wales remodelled it to resemble a Jacobean mansion. It has been likened to an oversize country hotel but remains a private home for the Royal Family. According to a letter in Country Life June 11 2008 the Duke of Edinburgh showed the letter writer a room full of framed press illustrations of the Duke's well known gaffes. Well adjusted is any man who can laugh at himself!

Sandringham owes its name to the greensand soil of the area, it was the sandy area of Dersingham village. Under the orders of the Prince of Wales roads were built, tenanted farms improved and trees planted. A stud was created and by 1890 the royal acres had become the best shooting estate in England with a regular annual bag of around twenty eight thousand birds. Today it comprises twenty thousand acres with annual events such as the hugely popular Sandringham Flower Show held on the estate.

SCOULTON MERE
There are numerous meres in Breckland. This one is privately owned with no public access. It was once the site of the rare great black-headed gull and gulls' eggs feature on the village sign. Red deer are said to inhabit the centre island.

Opposite: **SEA PALLING SUNSET**
The reefs were constructed with Scandinavian boulders 1993–97 for the Environment Agency. Gradually the beach is building up behind them, especially those which are set closer together and there has been no serious flooding or erosion since their installation.

SENNOWE

The house at Guist sits comfortably on its sloping site. It's the last great country mansion to be built in Norfolk (1908). The architect was George Skipper, described as 'Norfolk's answer to Lutyens'. He took the core of an eighteenth century house and created a magnificent home for the grandson of Thomas Cook founder of the travel company whose family still live there. The lake was dug with the aid of steam engines and a miniature railway.

SIDESTRAND

One look at the cliffs will demonstrate the effectiveness of wooden revetments on the beach. Where they are installed they reduce the force of the waves thereby halting the washing away of the cliff.

SNETTERTON

Based on the former airfield of Snetterton Heath, occupied by the USAF during WW2, the Snetterton Race Track has been there since 1951. Each lap is 1.952 miles with seven corners. The driving on the adjacent A11 sometimes mirrors that on the racetrack although the road has become much safer and less scary since the advent of the dual carriageway.

SOUTH OF SHERINGHAM
Today's patchwork of fields shows the diversity of crops in this predominantly arable area but the land has been farmed here since the Iron Age (about 600BC).

ST BENET'S

St Benet's (short for Benedict) was the only one of the monasteries not to be dissolved by Henry VIII. This strange little quirk of history arose because earlier the Abbey's Abbot had been appointed also as Bishop of Norwich, a move Henry must have later come to regret. To this day the Bishop of Norwich is also the Abbot of St Benet's and once a year arrives by river to conduct a service. The footings of the monastery including the stew ponds where fish were kept for winter food show up well from the air. The only remaining building is part of the gatehouse where inside, incredibly, a couple of centuries ago a windmill was built for grinding rapeseed for oil. No planning permission required then! Recent flood alleviation work has been undertaken on both sides of the river.

ST NICHOLAS, GREAT YARMOUTH

This is the largest parish church in England and much of it was built in the 13th century. Destroyed by fire during WW2 the church was rebuilt 1957–60 except for the original spire. There's much of the defensive mediaeval town wall still standing including three of the original fifteen towers.

The birthplace of Anna Sewell, author of 'Black Beauty', stands close by.

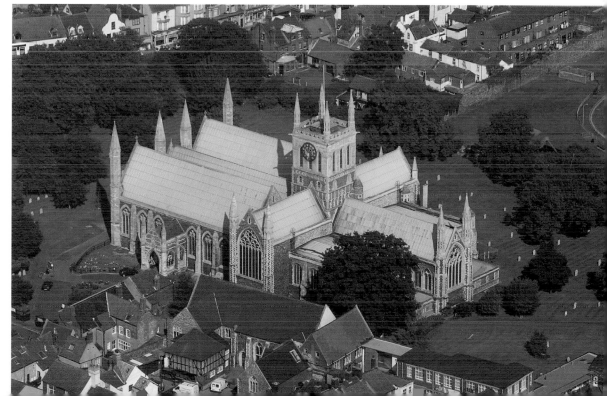

STIFFKEY HALL

The four towers and the footings of the quadrangular Great Hall are all that remain of the original Elizabethan Manor House built by Nathaniel Bacon in the sixteenth century. The next door church is perhaps best known for the activities of its one time vicar the Rev Harold Davidson who spent much of his incumbency in London 'working' with London prostitutes. He was unfrocked on the grounds of immorality in Norwich Cathedral 1932 although many local people believed him innocent. Life steadily got worse for him perhaps because of his poor judgement . He preached the gospel from inside an occupied lion's cage believing that his innocence would spare him. His mauled corpse proved him wrong.

STOKE HOLY CROSS MASTS

Britain's defences in WW2 owe much to the brilliant invention of the Chain Home transmitter masts of which the rear mast shown here was one. It has been preserved, the others have rusted away. Chain Home, developed at Bawdsey Manor in Suffolk by Robert Watson-Watt and his fellow scientists, enabled the path of enemy aircraft to be tracked by radar. The nearer mast belongs to BT and carries links to several transmission sites around Norfolk.

SWAFFHAM

Swaffham with its elegant Butter Cross (1783) is best known for its pedlar. It's stretching credulity to believe that a chapman (pedlar) from a little Norfolk town would just happen to meet someone on London Bridge telling him to go back home and find gold buried in his garden. One John Chapman, probably the same because the dates fit (around 1468), was possibly engaged in a bit of skullduggery whilst acting on behalf of Sir John Paston in the Caister Castle possession row against the Duke of Norfolk after Fastolf's death. How else could John Chapman explain his ill gotten gains acquired during the negotiations? Gold under an apple tree? Hardly likely. But nothing's all bad, the church gained a new aisle financed by him, he went down to posterity in a couple of pew end carvings and the town gained a story to put on their town sign.

But pedlars apart, Swaffham's second claim to fame since 1999 has been the Ecotech Centre with its eighty metre high wind turbine, the first multi megawatt wind turbine in the UK. It's possible to climb the 300 steps up a spiral staircase to the viewing platform. And on a more mundane subject W E Johns, writer of the 'Biggles' books whose hero's flying exploits delighted many small boys, started work as a Sanitary Inspector here in Swaffham!

SWAFFHAM RAILWAY ROUTES

From the air it's easy to spot railway lines old and current, except that in common with many Norfolk towns and villages after the radical prunings of the 1960s there are no current lines. The Swaffham – Dereham line is the curve to the left of picture. It closed in 1968. The Swaffham to Thetford line closed to passengers in 1964 and to freight in 1965.

SWANTON MORLEY

Grass runways are most often associated with pre-war airfields but RAF Swanton Morley, built at the start of WW2, accommodated tailwheel aircraft such as the de Havilland Mosquito, Bristol Blenheim and Airspeed Oxford all of which were designed to operate off grass strips. The airfield remained operational until the mid 1950s, latterly as an Air Signallers' School (A.S.S) whose mascot appropriately was a donkey. The signallers were flown in another tailwheel aircraft, the Avro Anson. In 1995 the RAF handed over the airfield to the Army and it became Robertson Barracks.

TERRINGTON ST CLEMENT

Some of the Fenland churches are almost cathedral-like in size and magnificence and reflect the prosperity of the area in the 14th century. Terrington St Clement is one of the best examples but there are others to rival it such as Walsoken, Walpole St Peter and West Walton. Terrington always has been at risk from flood and when in 1607 a dyke burst the villagers fled to the church tower for safety and were marooned there for several days being fed by boats from Kings Lynn. Dyke walls have been built here over the centuries to keep the sea at bay, the last being constructed by German prisoners of war 1914–18.

THETFORD

Nikolaus Pevsner, architectural historian writing in the 1970s said , "The great days of Thetford are over". In 869AD the Saxons set up camp here. As early as the eleventh century the town had eleven churches and a priory, in the twelfth century a second priory and a nunnery and before any of these, a castle had come and gone. Eight centuries later the buildings which made an impact on Thetford were very different in design and purpose. They were the rows and rows of houses of London overspill housing. Between 1951 and 1981 the town's population quadrupled. The people who moved into those houses were seeking a better quality of life much as Thomas Paine (1737–1809), Thetford's best known son, advocated on both sides of the Atlantic. His pamphlet 'The Rights of Man' and other writings and preachings branded him in this country as a subversive and in America (not yet the United States) as a prophet of better things which could be achieved for the ordinary man. Thetford eventually gave him recognition and a statue.

THETFORD CASTLE MOUND

Some say that the devil created this mound by dragging his foot along the ground and scraping his boot after he'd made the Devil's Dyke (an ancient roadway also known as the Launditch) at Weeting. Actually the mound is an iron age hill fort similar to that at Warham. It guarded against attackers entering from the River Little Ouse.

Opposite: **THETFORD FOREST**

Early morning mist in a Forestry Commission plantation. Not always has such a tranquil scene existed. Highwaymen stalked the road where the forest now stands. 'Gallows Hill' doesn't need much of an explanation.

THETFORD PRIORY

Cluniac monks built an abbey here in the twelfth century much like that at Castle Acre.

THETFORD: FIBROWATT POWER STATION

A power station has been built next to the River Little Ouse at Thetford to extract heat calories from poultry litter. It's one of three in the UK which together supply enough electricity for one hundred and fifty thousand homes. Not chicken feed.

THICKTHORN INTER-CHANGE

This is the junction of two of the busiest routes in Norfolk, the A11 Norwich to London and the A47 Great Yarmouth to Leicester roads. It's named after the nearby Thickthorn agricultural estate.

THOMPSON COMMON

In 1942 a large area (17,500 acres) north of Thetford including 3 complete parishes (Stanford, Tottington and West Tofts and parts of several others including Thompson) were commandeered by the Army as a Training Ground (STANTA = Stanford Training Area) in preparation for the D Day landings. The villages have never been handed back. So Mike Page had to be *very careful* not to stray into the Danger Area when taking this picture! Scenes were shot around here in the making of 'Dad's Army'. This is Breckland where the soil is light, where gorse and bracken flourish and rabbits and pingoes abound. Contrary to expectations pingoes are not wild strange creatures but small pools of water, relics of the Ice Age. Pockets of water were trapped beneath a frozen surface and became ice mounds. In summer the soil melted and slipped sideways leaving banks and exposing the water which stayed as small pools as here in the picture. There's an eight mile Great Eastern Pingo Trail starting at nearby Stow Bedon. The area is managed by the Norfolk Wildlife Trust.

TITCHWELL

Since 1973 the RSPB has helped create a diversity of wetland and coastal habitats here at Titchwell. Species attracted have included the marsh harrier, bittern, bearded tits and avocets, and the internationally important wintering wading birds. Recent coastal erosion has put the freshwater habitats under increasing pressure so the RSPB has begun a three-year programme to protect the reserve and its wildlife. Realigning the sea defences over a small part of the reserve and reinforcing the sea bank behind the brackish marsh should protect the freshwater habitat whilst allowing natural coastal processes over the rest of the site.

UPPER SHERINGHAM

Sheringham, the resort, grew up around the fishing village. Upper Sheringham, the village, came first and has a six hundred year old church. In the distance is Sheringham Hall, the house and grounds designed by Humphry Repton and adjacent to National Trust land. Weybourne village is in the far distance.

WALSINGHAM

Until the Reformation twelfth century Walsingham Priory was almost as popular a place of pilgrimage as Canterbury. There were several pilgrims' routes for example The Walsingham Way which originally was part of a Drove Road. Halting places such as a wayside chapel – there's one in the nearby village of Houghton St Giles – were where pilgrims chose often to proceed onwards barefoot, including Henry VIII. Only the Abbey gardens remain, access is through a fifteenth century gateway. The original buildings have been incorporated into an eighteenth century house known as Walsingham Abbey with the remains of the refectory with stone pulpit adjoining. There are modern churches built by the Anglican and Roman Catholic faiths, the former in Walsingham, the latter in Houghton St Giles.

WARHAM CAMP

Warham Hill Fort was built by the Iceni tribe sometime between 50 BC and AD 50. Hill forts are rare in Norfolk and there are only three others (South Creake, Narborough and Tasburgh). Warham is the only one with a double ditch. The walls are thirty feet high in some places, the site extends over three and a half acres. The land slopes down towards the River Stiffkey. The people who built the hill forts were wealthy enough to commission the making of decorative jewellery such as torcs. The prospect of finding such treasure excites those in possession of metal detectors today.

WAXHAM GREAT BARN

At one hundred and eighty feet this is the longest barn in Norfolk, built around 1580 as a granary by the Woodhouse family. They had made their money, as had so many others of the period, from the wool trade, i.e. they were 'broggers'. The barn was in danger of becoming derelict when Norfolk County Council and English Heritage rescued it in 1991 and replaced what was left of the corrugated iron roof with thatch. It now houses a colony of bats and a barn owl.

WAYLAND WOOD

This is a managed woodland where coppicing is practised to maintain a diversity of species. The story of the Babes in the Wood (based on possible truths) was set, four hundred years ago, in Wayland Wood. A wicked uncle living at nearby Griston Hall is due to inherit the wealth of his nephew and niece. He arranges for them to be killed in the wood. Readers will be glad to know that the wicked uncle came to a nasty end. Pictured also is the former airfield of RAF Watton and the town. The old railway line, (the straight line just above the wood) ran from Thetford to Swaffham but closed in 1964.

WEETING CASTLE

Here are the remains of a twelfth century moated hall where Hereward the Wake is said to have sought refuge when hiding from the Norman conquerors.

WELLS

Wells is today the first harbour northwards from Great Yarmouth since previous harbours at Salthouse, Blakeney, Cley and Wiveton gradually silted up once the marshes were drained for agriculture in the 17th century. There's a striking difference between the land to the left of the channel belonging to the Holkham Estate which was drained and embanked in the 19th century and the untouched saltmarshes of East Hills to the right. The ships bringing in coal and taking out grain no longer come and tie up at the quay and the town today relies heavily on tourism.

WELLS HARBOUR

Wells Quay with Dutch sailing barge 'Albatros'. There are occasions when the barge has difficulty negotiating the shallow channel.

132

WELNEY WASHES

Owned by the Wildfowl and Wetlands Trust since 1968, the Welney Washes are part of the River Ouse Washes. These were constructed by Dutch Engineer Vermuyden for the fourth Duke of Bedford (1630) to act as a flood plain in the complexity of water management in the Fens. Vermuyden built the Old Bedford River (left of picture) and the New Bedford River aka the Hundred Foot Drain (right) to facilitate the drainage of the River Great Ouse between Earith and Downham Market. Today the Welney Washes comprise over a thousand acres of wetland and provide a haven for wintering swans as well as being an SSSI and the most important lowland area of wet grassland for birds in Britain. There are hides where Bewick's and Whooper swans, widgeon, gadwall, teal, pintail and shoveller ducks all can be seen at close quarters. There's also a board walk, an Information Centre (near picture), a shop, a café and an Observatory.

WEYBOURNE

A steam engine from the North Norfolk Railway puffs through the beautiful countryside between Sheringham and Holt. Next to the village of Weybourne is a windmill and the wide open spaces of the Muckleborough Collection of military memorabilia from tanks downwards on the other side. When the wind is in the right direction it's possible to land a light aircraft here. The beach slopes steeply at this point which leaves the land vulnerable to attack from the sea owing to enough depth for enemy boats to get close in. Hence the rhyme *"He who would England win must first at Weybourne Hope (Hoop) begin"*.

In the 1930s there was an anti-aircraft artillery range here.

WHITLINGHAM

Whitlingham Country Park is one of the big success stories of the last ten years. It's Norwich's 'green lung', where a variety of physical activities can be enjoyed. In the 'Great Broad' (not a broad at all in the peat extraction sense but certainly a wide expanse of water) it's possible to sail, row, canoe and windsurf with both instruction and boat hire available. The Great and Little Broads were created by gravel extraction for Norwich's Southern ByPass.

WIGGENHALL ST GERMANS NEW PUMPING STATION

When completed later this year (2009) this will be the UK's largest pumping station. To the left of picture is the old pump which has been draining the land here in the Fens since 1934, to be dismantled once the new installation is up and running. The Middle Level Catchment area of which St Germans is part has been victim of wind erosion and peat shrinkage over centuries. The land is now below river level so water needs to be pumped up and away.

WISSINGTON BEET FACTORY

Built in 1925, this is the largest sugar beet processing factory in Europe but since 2005 has been engaged also in the development of bio-butanol using the by products of beet processing. The tomato producing glasshouses (top left) use the heat from the factory.

WOLFERTON STATION

The station, only two miles from Sandringham, was opened in 1863. To serve the large number of distinguished visitors a dedicated Royal Waiting Room was provided. Trains would have routed from London to Kings Lynn then reversed to continue the journey on to Wolferton. Nowadays the Queen travels in a special coach on a regular train service as far as Kings Lynn then on to Sandringham by car. Until recently special formalities had to be observed when the Queen entered the City of London so travelling from Liverpool Street station to Norwich would have been a bit of a performance. This ritual appears to have been abandoned when the Queen travels from the station today.

WOLTERTON HALL

Both Wolterton and Mannington Halls were built by Robert Walpole's brother Horatio and the Hall remains in the family. It's considered 'classical and austere and stands aloof across a wide park'. It endured military occupation during WW2 which left it in not entirely good shape but the present Lord Walpole is in the process of restoring it.

WORSTEAD FESTIVAL

The Worstead Festival has been an annual event for the last forty years. Initially its aim was to raise money for church repairs. The Festival is held in July each year and involves just about the whole village including the school. A School Inspector visiting the Festival in the 1970s remarked "I've never before had to *part with money* to enter a school!". The magnificent church, built from the proceeds of 15th century local worsted woollen cloth manufacture (note the spelling variation) retains its box pews.

WROXHAM: THE CAPITAL OF THE BROADS

It was here the holiday Hire Industry began in 1878 when John Loynes rented out his boats to those seeking a holiday in an area only recently 'discovered'. The 'Largest Village Store in the World' (Roys of Wroxham) actually mostly over the bridge in Hoveton – occupies most of the commercial buildings (foreground). Although the Boat Hire Industry is much smaller than it was fifty years ago nonetheless there's plenty of waterborne activity here in the summer.

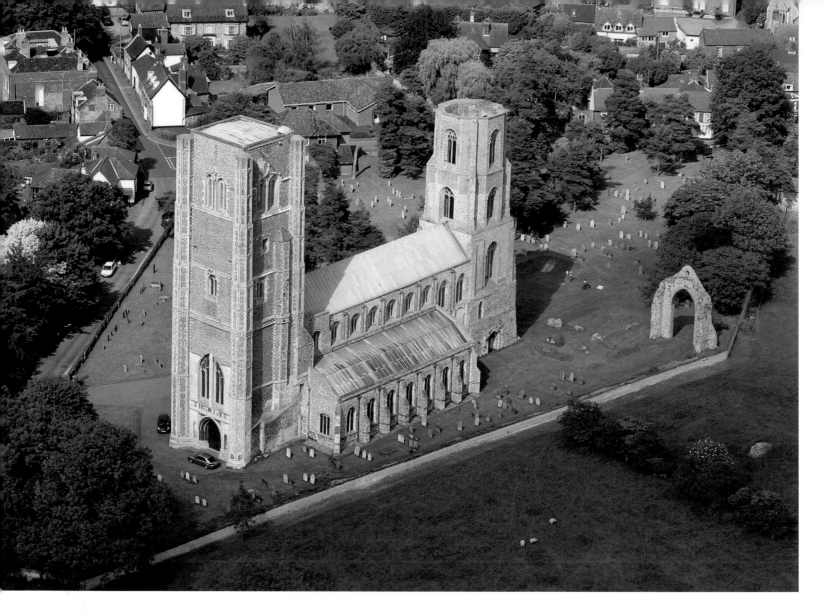

WYMONDHAM ABBEY

This small market town has several fine old buildings but none to compare with Wymondham Abbey. Begun in 1107 shortly after Norwich Cathedral, the building has witnessed turbulent times first as a Benedictine Priory, then in a conflict with Wymondham's townspeople. The townspeople, eventually, were able to claim part of the building as their parish church which it remains to this day. William Kett, brother of rebel and people's champion Robert who fought against the enclosure of common land in 1549, was hanged from the Abbey's West Tower (Robert suffered a similar fate from the top of Norwich Castle's Keep). It's worth looking inside the Abbey to see the magnificent altar screen designed by Ninian Comper as a War Memorial.

WYMONDHAM

To the west of the Abbey the land falls away to the diminutive River Tiffey and to the Mid Norfolk Railway whose visiting heritage diesel engines and steam locomotives draw enthusiastic passengers wanting to experience travel on the reopened line between Wymondham Abbey Station (created expressly for the MNR) and Dereham. There are plans to extend the line to County School Station, the railway station built to serve the Watts Naval Training School at North Elmham.

In what once was a compact market town several new housing estates have appeared in the last two decades and, despite fears that the infrastructure is not sufficient to support them, a further three thousand houses are planned.

YAXHAM

The Mid Norfolk Railway operates trains between Dereham and Wymondham on the line which stopped running a regular commercial service around 1988.

Here the train is being pulled by GWR 0–6–0PT number 9466 which has made brief visits to the MNR every year since 2006. The narrow gauge track in the background is operated by a separate group of enthusiasts and has been in place since the early 1980s. In the foreground is the old goods shed which now serves as an engineering works for the MNR.

ZOO AT BANHAM

There are a thousand animals in the thirty-five acres of Banham Zoo. It opened in 1968 with a collection of parrots and pheasants, now there's a very comprehensive list of animals including one of the finest collections of woolly monkeys in Europe. Snow leopards and other exotic and endangered species are recent attractions. In addition there's an Activities and Education Centre and animal encounter talks.

LATE EVENING OVER NORFOLK
If you're lucky enough to experience a hot air balloon ride take along a zoom lens for some terrific photographs. This is one of the best and quietest ways to see the Norfolk countryside. But direction is entirely dependent on the wind and it might take many trips to drift overhead all the places in this book!

BIBLIOGRAPHY

Bonwick Luke *Norfolk's Windmills* Bonwick Publishing 2008
Cattermole (Ed) *Wymondham Abbey* Wymondham Abbey Book Committee 2007
Cook Olive *Breckland* Robert Hale 1980
Dymond David *The Norfolk Landscape* Alastair Press 1990
Ekwall Eilert *Concise Oxford Dictionary of Place Names* Oxford 1977
Harrod Wilhelmine *The Norfolk Guide* Alastair Press 1988
Hutchinson Sheila *The Island (Haddiscoe Island)* S & P Hutchinson 2002
Jenkins Simon *England's Thousand Best Churches* Penguin Press 1999
Jenkins Simon *England's Thousand Best Houses* Penguin Press 2003
Kinsey Gordon *Pulham Pigs* Terence Dalton 1988
Malster Robert *Saved from the Sea* Terence Dalton 1974
Norfolk & Suffolk Aviation Museum Publication *Norfolk Airfields*
Pevsner Nikolaus *North West & South Norfolk* Penguin 1977
Pevsner Nikolaus *North East Norfolk & Norwich* Penguin 1976
Pocock Tom *Norfolk* Pimlico County Guides 1995
Shreeve & Stilgoe *The Round Tower Churches of Norfolk* Canterbury Press 2001
Smith Graham *Norfolk Airfields in the Second World War* Countryside 1994
Toulson Shirley *East Anglia* Whittet Books 1979
Wade Martins Susanna *A History of Norfolk* Phillimore 1997
Williamson Tom *England's Landscape – East Anglia* English Heritage 2006
Winkley George *The Country Houses of Norfolk* Tyndale 1968